THE RETURN OF THE CHERUB

SEQUEL TO MIRACLE - CONVERSATIONS WITH A CHERUB

N. SRINIVASA RAGHAVAN

BlueRose ONE.com
Stories Matter
NewDelhi • London

BLUEROSE PUBLISHERS
India | U.K.

BlueRose ONE.com
Stories Matter
NewDelhi • London

For permissions requests or inquiries regarding this publication, please contact:

BLUEROSE PUBLISHERS
www.BlueRoseONE.com
info@bluerosepublishers.com
+91 8882 898 898
+4407342408967

ISBN: 978-93-7139-658-5

Cover design: Daksh
Typesetting: Tanya Raj Upadhyay

First Edition: September 2025

Table of Contents

Prologue 1

PART– I 5

THE RETURN 5

You Are Not Alone 6

Repaying a Debt of Gratitude 12

Taking Stock 16

Part – II The Little One Speaks 18

Caregiving for the Elderly 19

Gurukulam Takes Wings– An Initiative by Mothers of Specially-Abled Children 26

Gurukulam Rising – A Caring and Compassionate Ecosystem 30

No Right or Wrong on the Continuum of Human Consciousness 33

Need for Institutional Care for the Specially-Abled 39

Engulfing Loneliness 43

Stalling Spiritual Progress 53

Preserving Our Spiritual Heritage 65

Flight to Redemption 71

Epilogue 83

Prologue

This offering is a sequel to my earlier book – Miracle – Conversations with a Cherub. The idea of writing Miracle started taking shape in the aftermath of my mother's demise. My first literary venture was a tribute to my mother titled "Amma – A Memoir of the Loveliest Woman I Knew". Her absence left a huge void in our lives, and my soul was seeking answers to questions that troubled me. It was then that the idea of Miracle took shape.

Miracle is a semi-fictionalized account of my late nephew, my late elder brother's eldest son. A lovely child of ethereal charm and beauty, which mirrored a beautiful and evolved soul inside. But as Fate would have it, the boy was born with a genetic disorder, for which there was no cure. Doctors didn't give the child not more than a dozen years.

The child was confined to bed, and couldn't even speak. But in these twelve lovely years (my life's best years as far as I am concerned), he wrought a transformation in all of us, particularly me. In fact, he didn't have to speak. His lovely, sparkling eyes, and his ebullient smile welcomed and embraced all. This was a lesson to all of us in unconditional love.

Miracle conjures up a story where the child appears, albeit in astral form, eighteen years after his passing, on a desultory summer's day in 2020; a time that was marked by my own struggles in coming to terms with my mother's loss. Thus began a daily rendezvous, wherein the Little One would appear unfailingly at his appointed hour, and engage me in conversations on Love, Friendship, Duty, Enlightenment, Impermanence, Letting Go, and many more nuggets of wisdom.

On 9th December 2024, the one person to whom I was clinging on to for dear life finished his earthly journey in the wee hours. I had lost my father. The enormity of this loss dawned on me after the thirteen-day ceremonies for my dear father had concluded. I was now all alone in this big, wide world (chosen to remain a bachelor and therefore have no immediate family). The first 45 days in the aftermath of my father's passing was extremely difficult for me. But gradually, I came to terms with what is inarguably the Law of Nature. The ensuing three to four months kept me busy attending to my father's financial affairs, and executing his Will. My father had made me the executor of his Will. Sometime, in the latter half of May 2025, this idea started gaining shape that I should write a sequel to Miracle – Conversations with a Cherub.

The Little One, sensing my loneliness and my deep sense of loss, chose to return again in his astral form, and engage me in gentle conversations, and in the process imparting precious wisdom to a wounded soul. I am a soul who is still on his evolutionary journey, and based on the karmic blueprint that I chose before I was born, I have learnt a few karmic lessons. But there are a lot many more karmic lessons that I have still to learn, or am struggling to learn based on my karmic blueprint. Lessons like detachment, struggles with my mortality, and my stalling spiritual progress would leave me despondent, and almost give up on my own self. In March 2025, I penned my father's memoir – Maryada Purushottam – The Making of Man. Being happy with how my father's memoir came up acted as a shot in the arm when the idea of a sequel to Miracle occurred to me.

I knew that there are a lot many more lessons that I have still got to learn, and who better to teach it to me than my Cherub. His real name was Navneet, and I used to affectionately call him Govinda. The reason for giving him the name of Govinda was that there was a striking resemblance between the little fellow and a picture of Lord Krishna we have in our Pooja room.

This book takes the audience on a fascinating journey wherein Govinda imparts me wisdom on areas of my life that I am still grappling with, and the many karmic lessons that I have still to learn. My struggles as a human being encapsulates the human condition, and therefore, anyone reading this book will find that there will surely be areas that will resonate with them. What appears at the outset as a fantastical tale really is a spiritual story whose narrative carries precious nuggets of wisdom to souls who are thirsting for guidance, and gaining in wisdom.

I hope my dear readers that after reading and putting down this book, you would have turned mellower, more compassionate, more empathetic, and a lot more wiser.

Pranaams.

N. Srinivasa Raghavan

PART – I

THE RETURN

You Are Not Alone

A new reality had dawned. The love, protection, and emotional security that is so very typical of parental profile, and that is almost taken for granted by a child, no matter how old he/she is, had practically disappeared for me from the face of the earth. My father, who I considered my ideal and my Maryada Purushottam, had cast off his mortal coil and merged into the Source from which we all originate from, and return to eventually. My mother had predeceased him, and I was clinging on emotionally to my father for dear life, momentarily oblivious to the fact that everyone born has got to die one day. I noticed his gradual decline in the last two to three weeks preceding his demise, and it had alerted me to the fact that he was nearing the end of a long, glorious and illustrious life.

Two years ago, he lay in bed seriously ill, and remained so for a better part of five months. But The Divine, in whom my father had implicit faith, interceded on his behalf to engineer a miraculous recovery, when I had almost given up hope that he will come through. Beginning March 2023 and going on till his demise on 9th December 2024, I had become his caregiver. This period was marked by a deep bond of love (not that it didn't exist before, but which I wasn't aware of) between father and son, and I remember telling him candidly on one occasion that I never knew that I loved him so much. The act of caregiving was an act of redemption for all my faults and shortcomings, and it was as if my father had willed to live on for these two years to wring in a personal transformation in me.

In these two years, I had learnt to see the world through the eyes of the old and the infirm, and the need to be sensitive, empathetic and compassionate to the physical challenges of aging. But there was no miraculous comeback the second time round, and my father attained the feet of The Lord in the wee hours of 9th December 2024. I hadn't realized till then that he had prepared me for life after him, for I had reined in my emotions, and had set myself down to doing what was required all alone, as my sister was battling health issues and couldn't be by my side.

Carrying my father home in an ambulance, informing the family priest to conduct his cremation rites, booking a slot at the crematorium were all done without a hint of an emotional meltdown. After his thirteen-day ceremonies had been attended to, I finally came face to face with the bottomless void that I was staring at. The thought and the feeling finally sunk in that I was all alone in this wide world, without the love, care and support of my parents any more.

As I had more or less retired from my active career, and had chosen to remain a bachelor, this engulfing loneliness started hurting more and more. I was at home all by myself, and sauntering into my parents' room would cause fond and precious memories of Mom and Dad to flood my mind. Life had become barren with nothing to look forward to as Existence blessed me with the promise of a new day. There were days when I would feel a knot in my stomach after a few mouthfuls of food, and would somehow go through the motions of eating a meal. It was at precisely this emotionally vulnerable moment that I recalled the sage counsel of my mother who would always ask me as to what I would do after they (Mom and Dad) are gone. But that was the time when I was still in my mid-forties, and had been very confident that life could be lived all alone.

If days were marked by nostalgia and the struggle to shake off the engulfing loneliness, sleep would be at a premium come night time. I was anyway a light sleeper, and sleep would hardly settle in as thoughts of my parents would fill my mind. It was on one such night that I had gone to bed hoping that sleep would overtake me, and give my body and mind time to rejuvenate in order to face a new day with hope and optimism. Sleep was again very light, as I tossed and turned in my bed.

It was in such a state of mind that I thought that I was dreaming in which someone with a dulcet-like, sweet and childlike voice was seeming to assure me that "You are not alone". I presumed that I was dreaming, ignoring the almost entreating voice of the child. That childlike reassurance resonated again and again, and finally I opened my eyes to know whether the voice was real, or my mind was playing tricks with me.

As I opened my eyes in the darkness of the night, what I witnessed came as a balm to soothe the hurt that my heart and soul were enduring. Piercing through the darkness, and suspended in midair like an almost holographic apparition was my little fellow, my nephew. His cherubic countenance with that characteristic ruddy complexion shone in contrast to the enveloping darkness. There was a twinkle in his eyes, and an almost mirthful smile played on his lovely lips. He was dressed in his favourite gold-coloured printed silk shirt paired with green shorts, and white and red sandals.

I still wasn't sure whether all this was a beautiful dream, or reality playing out in front of my eyes. As if to confirm my misgivings, I asked haltingly, "Is it my Govinda?". Pat came the reply, "Yes, I am indeed your little Govinda". This gentle, infantile reassurance caused the stoic exterior that I had put on successfully in the wake of my father's demise to break, and tears of relief started flowing down my cheeks at having been alleviated of my loneliness, which had started gnawing at my heart and soul."

Five years ago, he had appeared in his astral form in identically the same fashion, and engaged me in invigorating conversations to lift my spirits and give my life a sense of direction in the aftermath of my mother's loss. Having lost my father, and struggling to cope with his loss, I had hit a cul-de-sac, not knowing what next step I had to take to face up to, and attain some form of closure with regard to my parents' demise.

He seemed to read my mind, and resumed in his cuckoo-like sweet voice. "I knew that the time was ripe for me to come again to give you a fair amount of reassurance, console you on Grandma and Grandpa's passing over, that their end was timely and pre-ordained as per their karmic blueprint that they had chosen for themselves, that you did the best you could for them that any loving child could do, and to help you come to terms that they both lived a noble and purposeful life, before closing out their life's journey. But above all, I have appeared once again after a five-year hiatus to reassure you that you are not alone, and that I have been keeping a watchful gaze on my dear uncle. Rest assured Balu, you are not alone". As if to prove his point, his astral form changed into a corporeal, physical form, he came close to me and held me in a warm embrace, and stroked my head with his gentle, little hands to calm down the storms of grief that had been raging in my heart. Once his gentle embrace and reassuring touch had calmed me down reasonably, he addressed me again in his characteristic gentle voice. "It has been an emotionally overwhelming period for you. Enough for today. From tomorrow onwards, I shall appear to you just before you retire for the day, and converse with you, hoping to answer many of the questions that are still haunting you. Good night for now. Rest well. And look forward to a new day with renewed hope and optimism". Saying so, Govinda's astral form gradually merged into the ambient darkness.

As I closed my eyes gratefully, I almost instantaneously fell sleep. After a long, long time, sleep came as a gentle balm, temporarily but effectively making me oblivious to the challenges of the real world. This was a role reversal that I never knew would transpire one day, a little child consoling me, and putting me to sleep. A role that I had played for my nephew almost three-and-a-half decades ago.

Repaying a Debt of Gratitude

The next day, at the appointed hour, just before retiring for the night, I had switched off the lights, when the Little One materialized in the darkness, looking resplendent and beautiful. It was a beauty which didn't pander to your senses, but touched your soul.

As I seated myself on my bed, and readied myself to hear the Little One speak, Govinda addressed me thus, "Our first order of business should be to help you achieve emotional closure on Grandpa's passing. It isn't a time for grieving. He lived a full life. A life of ninety years embellished by truth, nobility, generosity of spirit, and total commitment and the pursuit of excellence in one's duty. Along with Grandma, he was a very generous host, and shaped the careers and lives of many, within and outside the family. He lived his life in conformance with his Aaradya, Maryada Purushottam Shri Ram, and weathered many a storm in his life with courage, grace, and fortitude. He exemplified the highest ideal of Karma

Yoga taught by Lord Krishna. Gave his all to the performance of his duty, and learning to be content with whatever came his way.

His faith in The Almighty was unshakeable. Even in the close to two years following his miraculous recovery in March 2023, he had become very weak. But his strong mind and steely determination made him adhere to his prayer routine comprising two hours in the morning, and two hours in the evening without fail, till ten days before his demise.

I saw you advising Grandpa that in case he found it difficult to say his prayers, he could lie down on his bed, and keep saying "Govinda, Govinda", another name for The Lord, and calling out which The Lord responds almost instantaneously.

And since you gave me the name Govinda, it was as well a call to me. How could I not respond to Grandpa's soulful call. Grandpa was the one who set aside his grief, bathed my body, wrapped me in a dhoti, applied the religious mark of Sri Vaishnavism on my forehead, and prepared me for my final journey. How could I not be there for Grandpa, who I consider the noblest among men. I kept vigil by his side, ensuring that for one so noble, his passing over was graceful without pain and discomfort.

This was the family that gave me an abundance of love, affection and care, as I lived out my twelve years in a disabled body. And Grandpa was a strong pillar of support to Mom and Dad as they dealt with my debilitating condition in every which way they could.

You kept vigil over Grandpa in the physical realm, while I watched over him from the spiritual realm, invisible to you all, but very much by Grandpa's side. And I interceded with The Lord to grant Grandpa's soul a release in the Brahmamuhurtam time (4:00 am - 6:00 am) on Shuklapaksha Navami (the ninth day of the waning phase of the moon. The very day in the month of Chaitra that the world celebrates the birthday of Lord Rama). I knew Grandpa wished nothing more than complete his earthly journey on the auspicious Navami day, and The Lord acceded to my supplication.

You did everything a child could do for his aging parents, more so for Grandpa, as you became his caregiver in his last two years. Grieve not, Balu. Everyone who is born has to die one day, and what should comfort your soul is the fact that Grandpa's passing over was very, very blissful. The Lord never forsakes his flock, especially those who live a life of righteousness in accordance with His teachings. He sent me to ensure a dignified end to Grandpa's earthly journey. I was witness to Grandpa's last 6 days before his passing, and he passed over peacefully and gracefully without any accompanying pain and discomfort.

As you move on in your life, you should every moment celebrate Grandpa's life, and do everything possible to preserve and carry forward his precious legacy. And the first step you took was in writing his Memoir, "Maryada Purushottam - The Making of Man".

Hearing the Little One's words of reassurance greatly comforted my grieving soul, and as tears of gratitude streamed down my cheeks, Govinda came close to me, wiped my tears, gently patted me with his little hands, and held me close to his bosom.

"Have I finally helped you achieve emotional closure?", asked Govinda in his characteristic sweet and gentle voice. "Yes, Govinda", I said. "My heart and soul have finally found peace hearing you speak. I am sure the period of grieving has finally ended, thanks solely to your beneficence. My salutations to you, Govinda".

After hearing me speak, Govinda addressed me, " Enough for tonight. Saying so, he bade me goodbye, and merged into the enveloping darkness.

Taking Stock

What I yearned for most at the end of an eventful or uneventful day was to see the beautiful form of the Little One. He was my Guruvayurappan (the name given to the child form of Lord Krishna worshipped in his glorious temple in Guruvayoor).

My rendezvous with the Little One materialized with clockwork precision. On Day 3 of our conversations, he asked me, "How have you been over the last five years? Not that I don't know, but I wish to hear from you a first-person account of how you spent the last five years". There was an almost half-mischievous smile playing on his lips, as he waited on me to recount my narrative of the time since our last set of conversations.

I hesitated a while before starting to respond to the Little One's kind enquiries. "I think I have done nothing of note in the five years since the time we last conversed. There is very little to show by way of growth either in the intellectual or spiritual domain. I think I have essentially frittered away my time. Five years have meandered along aimlessly. I haven't been able to professionally upgrade myself. My spiritual progress has more or less stalled. I have tried in vain, and failed in triumphing over my human instincts. To put it succinctly, my life of the last five years can best be expressed as one step forward, and two steps back. There is an utter sense of dejection and worthlessness at not having registered any progress at all. Pray instruct me as to what I need to do. I am completely lost. And am all ears, and your willing disciple."

Govinda heard me out earnestly, and gave his answer in a one-line aphorism to ponder over before resuming our conversation the next night. He said in his dulcet-like voice, "How do you wish to see the world and yourself, as a glass half full, or a glass half empty?". With this parting shot, he gave me his characteristic big smile accompanied by the twinkle in his eyes, and merged into the night.

Part – II
The Little One Speaks

Caregiving for the Elderly

It was now a question of finishing all my chores for the night and waiting for the Little One with bated breath. And the Little One didn't disappoint. What more could I ask for!! The love of my life unfailingly appearing before me, and engaging me in illumining conversations. He began in his customary sweet and gentle tone.

"Balu, let us converse today on something very close to your heart; the subject of caregiving for the elderly, in particular, one's own parents, as they battle with Time, and the infirmities of old age. Let me put you front and centre into this conversation, and tell you how you fared in this very important role for every child as its parents gather on in years.

Let's begin with you calling time on your career early to spend quality time with Grandma and Grandpa. It was a very brave and courageous decision, buttressed by love and care for Grandma and Grandpa. You lovingly took on the routine household chores of buying groceries, running errands, and taking Grandma and Grandpa for their regular reviews with their doctors. Four years passed off happily before Grandma had her fall, and fractured her right humerus, and one of her lower spinal vertebrae. While surgery to her right humerus was successfully performed, given her age and osteoporosis, she was advised complete bed rest for her spinal vertebra to heal. All through her confinement to bed, you did everything possible for Grandma in terms of arranging an attender for her at home, arranging for a special injection for her to strengthen her bones, arranging for her periodic review by her orthopedic surgeon by arranging for an ambulance for her to be transported comfortably to the hospital, and bringing her back home. And finally getting her admitted to a rehab centre for physiotherapy, counseling and complete care.

Sadly, just after spending four days at the rehab centre, Grandma breathed her last. I have in my short life of twelve years never come across a woman so gentle, so dignified, and so compassionate. She was my childhood companion, and kept me in good spirits with her singing me lullabies, distracting me with simple games, feeding me, and putting me to sleep. All this she would do till my mother was at office. The moment mother returned home from office; she would pick me up in her arms and take me to her room.

Her passing away was a loss borne equally by you and Grandpa. I could see days when you struggled with Grandma's loss, and confessing to Grandpa that you are unable to deal with her loss, and Grandpa gently consoling you that you need to give it time to bear Grandma's loss, and achieve some kind of emotional closure.

And right through Grandpa's illness from October 2022 – March 2023, you bravely took on the caregiving duties for Grandpa, initially helped by my Athai (paternal aunt), and my granduncle and grandaunt. Till end of February 2023, it was a collaborative effort of taking care of grandpa with you, aunt, and my granduncle and grandaunt sparing no effort, and leaving no stone unturned.

Beginning March 2023, you solely took on the caregiving responsibilities for grandpa, as my aunt and my younger grandparents had to return to their respective homes to take care of their own families. Taking grandpa for tests and regular reviews by his gastroenterologist and nephrologist, and also starting off Ayurvedic treatment for his condition, and taking him almost every month for a review by his Ayurvedic doctor were tasks that you lovingly undertook for grandpa.

In between the caregiving, you and aunt planned to celebrate grandpa's landmark 90th birthday celebrations by inviting close family for the occasion. This was possibly the last time grandpa gifted each attendee and blessed them. And there was a hospitalization that he needed for Hypoproteinemia, a typical symptom of which is swollen legs, indicative of a malfunctioning liver. He was given three units of albumin, and discharged from hospital after being there for three days. This was mid-August 2024.

Beginning the third week of November 2024, signs of decline in grandpa's condition were conspicuous. And roughly two weeks before his passing, you kept a hawk-like vigil on grandpa, as his already slow gait had further slowed down, and you had to put your arm around his shoulder to help him move about at home.

Beginning 4th December, he was confined to bed, but was conscious. And from the 5th morning, he kind of went into a deep sleep, and stopped responding to calls. All these were signs of grandpa's body gradually shutting down. And to ensure that he got round the clock care, you got him admitted to Care Hospitals, Banjara Hills, where he breathed his last in the early morning hours of 9th December.

To lose one parent itself is a big blow for a child to bear, however old the child may be. To lose the other remaining parent is a double whammy, leaving the child to face a colossal emotional void difficult to deal, and come to terms with. And since you had chosen to remain a bachelor, the distractions of attending to your own family that would have taken your focus off, albeit temporarily of grandpa's loss, was also not there.

Here you were, all alone, and struggling with the huge emotional void of having lost both your parents. And I was watching how you struggled bravely, especially in the first forty-five days since grandpa's passing. But gradually, you came to terms with grandpa's loss and learnt to deal with occasions when you would land in an emotional trough.

Now, going forward, what is the best way do you think of dealing with this huge emotional void, and the ensuing loneliness." Govinda gently put this poser to me and waited for me to respond. I said haltingly, "Govinda, I am completely lost, and just do not know how to deal with the harsh reality of having lost my parents. You be my guide, and tell me what is the best way forward".

Govinda now resumed in his characteristic sweet and gentle voice. "The best way of dealing with losing grandma and then grandpa, and the ensuing emotional void is to spare some of your time to caregiving for the elderly. There are many an old age home where old couples spend their final years in the care of staff at these old age homes. Some old age homes are professionally run, and cost a lot, which the well to do can afford for their ageing parents. But there are old age homes, which are run solely with an eye on pecuniary benefit, and in the process compromising on good ventilation and sunlight, which are so essential for the health of the elderly.

Whether professionally-run old age homes or otherwise, what is essentially missing for the elderly here is the emotional context, where somebody sits down with them, enquiring about their well-being, shares a cheerful conversation, and runs small errands for them. This is all that the elderly look for. They yearn to feel that sense of belonging that warms their hearts, and all that they desire is for someone to sit down with them, talk to them, enquire about how they are doing, and in return receive bounteous blessings from them.

Why don't you devote at least some hours of one day of your weekend to spend at an old age home bringing cheer and succour to the elderly. Caring for the elderly who aren't your parents is a nobler act than caring for one's own parents, as altruism triumphs over ties of blood. It will to a great extent compensate for grandma's and grandpa's loss, which is hurting you so much. Some old couple may see a son in you, as their own children, who because of work and vocation, are far away from them, and unable to relocate back, as their own families have established roots in a foreign land. Please do give my suggestion a try, and see for yourself", chimed in Govinda.

I replied. "Why didn't such a noble thought ever cross my mind? I was so consumed by my own grief and deep sense of loss that I failed to appreciate that there could be people, especially the elderly, who could be worse off than me, and who need my kind attention. I am firm in my conviction that caring for the elderly by giving them time one day of the weekend will go a long way in alleviating my loneliness, and helping me reconnect with grandma and grandpa by serving the elderly. This has come as a revelation to me. I thank you Govinda from the bottom of my heart, and express my deep gratitude to you for having shown me the way. I am going to put your suggestion immediately to work, and am going to identify an old age home where I am going to serve the elderly for a few hours on one day over the weekend."

Govinda looked at me with his all-knowing smile, and said, "I knew you would take to my suggestion like a duck to water. I am very happy that your progression to caring for the elderly was spontaneous, and not laboured at all. With this he bade me goodbye, promising to meet me the next night at the same time. With this loving assurance, he melted into the enveloping darkness.

Gurukulam Takes Wings– An Initiative by Mothers of Specially-Abled Children

After Govinda had manifested himself at the appointed hour the next night, he addressed me thus. "I am going to talk about something that is very dear and close to our heart. Yes, I wish to talk today on a very noble initiative by my mother and Supriya aunty, both sharing a common destiny of being mothers to specially-abled children. The subject is Gurukulam, the school for the specially-abled, and children with special learning needs.

Gurukulam is a labour of love, born out of the empathy that only mothers of specially-abled children can have. When doors of mainstream society are slammed shut on these lovely children, and schools for normal children bluntly refuse to admit them, let alone take the trouble of starting a separate section for specially-abled children, mothers of specially-abled children are left in a near-hopeless situation, not knowing the road ahead for their children. It is out of such depths of despair that Gurukulam was born.

As the response of corporates ranged from rank indifference to not even lending an ear to hear the case for supporting an institution for the specially-abled, and having a very blinkered view of their CSR (Corporate Social Responsibility) mandate, and refusing to show flexibility and resilience to supporting smaller institutions committed to the cause of the specially-abled, my mother and Supriya aunty refused to give up. They pooled their own limited resources, and reached out to the extended family for whatever they could contribute.

What began in a small way in a garage with five specially-abled children has now grown to fifty children accommodated across two buildings of Gurukulam, with thirty special educators and support staff, all committed to making Gurukulam work with clockwork efficiency.

Funds have always been a challenge for Gurukulam, what with the advent of Covid eating away into the corpus of the school, which was required to pay for fixed expenses such as rent, power and lighting, and salaries of the teaching and support staff. And yet undeterred by this, my mother and Supriya aunty soldiered on, putting their faith in The Divine that has shown a guiding light to the school, and sustain it for the six years that it did.

When there would be question marks over how salaries and other monthly expenses were going to be met given the severe working capital crunch, a Good Samaritan would invariably stop by at the school, enquire about its vision and mandate, and consequently make a contribution, which would help tide over the pressing need of meeting the expenses of the school and keep it going.

Balu, I would like to point out that these aren't random acts of kindness, but the Hand of Providence is very much at play. And since the entire staff, including the founder mothers of the school have upheld the highest ideals of Karma Yoga, The Divine would nudge a Good Samaritan here, and a Good Samaritan there to come and help Gurukulam tide over its financial challenges. These acts of many Good Samaritans may to the lay observer appear as random acts of kindness, but a discerning eye and an introspective soul sees The Divine orchestrating these seeming random acts of kindness by these Good Samaritans, who seem to appear out of nowhere. This is what I would call the mechanics of altruism.

In conclusion, all I wish to say is that when a noble initiative is undertaken with the right intention, The Divine steps in to bear our burden, remove obstacles, and paving the way for the institution to flourish."

With these parting words, Govinda bade me goodbye, promising to meet me the next day. And in the next moment, he had merged into that dimension that is beyond the human eye.

Gurukulam Rising – A Caring and Compassionate Ecosystem

My rendezvous with Govinda had now become part of my daily routine. Come 10:00 pm, I will be waiting for the arrival of the Little One to illumine me with his enlightening conversations. And the Little One never disappointed even once.

After materializing before me, and rendering the ambient surroundings luminescent by his glowing presence, he continued with the topic of the day before, but gave a different perspective to the successful running of the school. He addressed me thus.

"Do you know, Balu what is the secret of Gurukulam successfully running for six straight years, in spite of the odds stacked heavily against it. No proper school-like building, no playground for the children to play in, a fund crunch encountered invariably every month, and yet, in spite of these overwhelming constraints, what is the secret of Gurukulam running so well. Here is my take on the success of Gurukulam.

The secret to Gurukulam's success is the unstinted devotion and commitment of the teaching and support staff to doing their duty, and more important, a deep love for the specially-abled children. In the current age where material pulls and pressures can lead a resource away from his/her current place of employment to more greener pastures, it is singularly interesting and fascinating to know that this special group of educators and support staff at Gurukulam have forsaken the lure of mammon, and continue doing their best for the school.

I have watched over the affairs of the school with great love and interest, and I can say with a lot of pride that this special group is at the heart of the success of Gurukulam. They have evolved into a tightly knit group, and have become family for my mother and Supriya aunty, and for many other families with specially-abled children.

I would rather stick my neck out, and proclaim that it isn't ties of blood that define a family, but rather, the coming together of likeminded souls, and staying steadfast by each other in trying times that goes to define a family. Grandpa lived by the ideal of Vasudaiva Kutumbakam (the whole world is my family), and it is so reassuring to see his legacy being continued by this very special group of educators and support staff, though most of them have little or no knowledge of Grandpa. A golden legacy needs no conscious effort for its perpetuation, but lives off its own divine energy, and finds avenues and opportunities for its continuance.

I am sure you, mother and Supriya aunty are seized of this very pressing requirement to keep this group together, and do whatever is required to take good care of them. This should be a fascinating case study for HR of large, cash-rich IT and pharma organizations, who are clueless about creating, motivating and retaining a committed group in spite of a hefty compensation package, and other financial inducements. They should spend a day at Gurukulam to understand human dynamics in greater depth than the shallow understanding of human nature that they currently possess", he concluded with a chuckle. With these fascinating insights into how committed groups feed off each other and stay together, notwithstanding the lack of commensurate rewards, he bade me good night, promising to meet me again the next night.

No Right or Wrong on the Continuum of Human Consciousness

After he had lighted up the night with his incandescent presence, the Little One still continued to talk about Gurukulam, the institution that seemed to engage his attention and energies the most. He said, "I will now talk about something that has been gnawing at your heart for a very long time. It is concerning the lack of empathy, and consequently, the lack of financial support for Gurukulam from those whose pockets are deep, and who could certainly make a big difference by providing financial support, and ensure that Gurukulam is in for a long innings.

Let us start at the efforts you made on this front. I remember you sending mails to Tata Trusts, and the Azeem Premji Foundation, making an impassioned plea for financial support for Gurukulam, and requesting an opportunity for hearing out the trustees of Gurukulam, and if they found the trustees making a compelling case, they could then contemplate the mode and quantum of financial support to be extended.

You wrote with high hopes. And ironically, the response was a deafening silence. Not even a polite response, communicating a refusal to support. Suspecting that your mails to these institutions would have got filtered out straight into the junk folder, you changed your strategy by writing a letter, printing it out, and sending it by courier to the Infosys Foundation. The founder members were middle class, and you nurtured a fond hope that this time round, the plea for financial help would find resonance with the Infosys Foundation. But unfortunately, the results were no different than the earlier attempts.

You then came to know from one of your seniors that CSR arms of organizations have a set mandate of what and how much they wish to channelize their funds to CSR initiatives. The mandate is set in stone, and these CSR arms of organizations have a rather blinkered vision of Corporate Social Responsibility, refusing to deviate from their CSR blueprint, which focuses more on doing things at a national level, and not considering even the deserving cases of smaller organizations like Gurukulam. This revelation came as a big disappointment.

And then came the role of the extended family. There were a few in the extended family, who given the fact that they made it big in their respective careers owing to the dint of their hard work and The Almighty's grace somehow continued living in a bubble, quite oblivious to the world around them. Even a small fraction of their contribution would have meant something very significant for Gurukulam, but the simple fact is this wasn't a priority for them, and never was on their radar to garner their immediate attention.

Balu, deep down in your heart, you were deeply hurt by this indifference, and wondered how the needs of Gurukulam could be brought into the collective consciousness of the extended family, and that too of their own volition. Quite often, you were privy to conversations wherein large sums of money were contributed to social causes, but wasn't funding Gurukulam also a social cause equally worthy of their kind consideration? And yet out of a sense of dignity, and a modicum of self-respect, mother and you never broached the issue of funding to the extended family, especially to those more than capable of making a significant contribution to Gurukulam.

It was left to the phlegmatic temperament of Supriya aunty who took it upon herself of canvassing for sponsors and funding for the fundraising musical concert that was being planned to contribute to the corpus of Gurukulam. The second fundraiser for Gurukulam was a grand musical concert by large hearted and generous singers and musicians from the Tamil and

Malayalam film industry, who did the concert for free. You were there for the concert as well, albeit for a short while, as you were feelings the effect of extreme physical and mental fatigue. The fact that the concert generated a goodly amount after accounting for expenses of the concert is heartening, and it should stand Gurukulam in good stead for some time to come.

Now, I will tell you something that you should remember till your very end. Stop being judgmental of people. Everyone who comes here as an incarnated soul comes with his/her own karmic blueprint, which contains the life lessons, or karmic lessons that they have come here to learn. You are learning your life lessons according to the karmic blueprint that you chose before you became an embodied soul. The fact that you operate out of a certain level of empathy and compassion for a cause close to your heart doesn't necessarily mean that others have to follow suit. They are doing and acting with full conviction based on their own respective karmic blueprints and karmic lessons that they have come here to learn, and are learning.

All the embodied souls here on earth are at various stages in their evolutionary journey on the continuum of human consciousness. This is very much like your experiences in school. You would recall how some students were extra bright, and could learn abstract and difficult concepts with relative ease, while others took a little more time to learn the same concepts. All students are equally competent, but based on their mental capacities, learn at their own pace. The evolutionary journey of the embodied souls is very similar. They are learning their karmic lessons at their own chosen pace based on their karmic blueprint. There should absolutely be no difference between a soul that evolves quicker, albeit undergoing emotional and mental hardships vis-à-vis souls who evolve at their own chosen pace.

The Divine does indeed place enough opportunities in the path of every soul to recognize and grab to quicken the pace of their evolutionary journey. Some blessed souls who have gradually downsized their egos, and have emptied themselves are open to receive Divine Grace, and are able to see, recognize and latch on to these opportunities, and use them to quickly climb the ladder of their spiritual evolution. But there are a lot many souls who are trapped by their ego, and are attending to all the trappings of the material world, with the mind and the ego goading them on. At some stage, they will have to jump off the bandwagon, but when that moment arrives is left to the individual soul. If they are willing to step back from the rat race of the material world, and introspect just a wee bit every day, this opportunity to step off the treadmill of the material world will come sooner rather than later.

So, in conclusion, learn to accept with gratitude whatever quantum of assistance comes to Gurukulam from anyone, irrespective of their economic capability, and their evolved human sensibilities. They are not to be judged, for there is Providence to judge them. Have I addressed something that has been hurting inside of you?", asked Govinda, with his trademark impish smile and a glint of mischief in his eyes.

I had no words to thank Govinda for this life-altering lesson. I said, "Govinda, you have opened my eyes to a new way of seeing the world. A view that is non-judgmental and based on a deep sense of gratitude. And a view that has finally come to understand the human condition. Accept everyone the way they are, without the need to form judgments and jump to conclusions. This is the greatest spiritual lesson that you have taught me. I am sure this is going to have a transformative impact on me, and quicken the pace of my soul's evolutionary journey. Thank you, Govinda from the bottom of my heart", and I bowed in deep reverence before the Little One.

With a beatific and mischievous smile that only The Divine One can pull off, Govinda waved me goodbye, and became one with the darkness of the night.

Need for Institutional Care for the Specially-Abled

I have never looked forward to anything with as much enthusiasm and excitement as hear Govinda speak. The sheer joy of hearing the Little One speak surpassed all human experiences for me. With these thoughts lingering in my mind, I sat cross-legged on my bed close to the appointed hour, when Govinda would mark his arrival. And he didn't disappoint. He appeared before me, looking radiant, and addressed me thus.

"Today, we will continue our conversation still on the subject of Gurukulam, but from a different perspective. The anxiety that is uppermost in the minds of parents of specially-abled children is who will look after them when they are gone. For families that have a normal child along with a specially-abled child, it is realistic for parents to assume that the normal elder or younger sibling will take on the responsibilities of caring for his specially-abled sibling, provided the parents have taken extra care of sensitizing their normal child that it is its bounden moral duty to attend to the well-being of his/her specially-abled sibling.

But for families where there is no other sibling around, like in mother's case, where she lost me first, followed by father, the concern and anxiety assume greater significance of who will attend to Arvind, my younger sibling after her time. This is a very sensitive issue on which I wish to speak to you, and where you have a very important role to play.

Institutional care for the specially-abled is a very important matter demanding our urgent attention. For this to become a reality, what is required is policy-level changes initiated by the Government, backed by adequate budgetary support for building and sustaining institutions for the specially-abled.

With an empathetic PMO willing to lend an ear to the common citizenry, the first step that you can take is to write to the PMO on its online portal, sensitizing the Government on the necessity of institutional care for the specially-abled. Once the right amount of awareness is brought upon the Government, the next step for Government will be to onboard special educators like my mother, and elicit their views on how institutions for the specially-abled should take shape, the kind of facilities that these institutions ought to have, trained, empathetic and caring staff, who have the wherewithal to handle the specially-abled firmly and compassionately. These institutions should ideally be nestled in the lap of nature, having a calming effect on the minds of the specially-abled, especially the autistic ones, who sometimes get hyperactive, and for whom natural environs can have a calming effect. These institutions should have all the necessary infrastructure for occupational and vocational therapy, where the specially-abled can be trained, and whatever useful commodities they produce can in turn be sold back to society at a nominal profit, that will in turn go back to the institution.

This is a Herculean task, first to bring awareness at the level of Government, then society at large, and finally, to the extended family as well. You will have to use the power of your pen, and leverage the ubiquitous print and electronic media, as also social media to create this awareness, impressing upon Government and citizenry the urgency of the task at hand.

I entrust you with this very important task, and I am confident that your sustained campaign will finally resonate in the corridors of power, and bring in the required policy changes and budgetary support for institutions for the specially-abled, while at the same time educating and bringing in the required empathy and compassion amongst the general public to the needs of the specially-abled.

My dream is to see Gurukulam evolve into such an institution, providing a safe haven for the specially-abled, where their safety, security and well-being is a given, apart from providing caregiving to the specially-abled, and training them in occupational and vocational therapy, thus ensuring they contributing meaningfully to society. Such an institution can best be exemplified by Thomas Gray's immortal lines from his poem, "Elegy Written in a Country Churchyard", considered to be the acme of English poetry.

> "Far from the madding crowd's ignoble strife
>
> Their sober wishes never learned to stray
>
> Along the cool sequestered vale of life
>
> They kept the noiseless tenor of their way."

Engulfing Loneliness

As I settled myself to hear the gentle discourse of the Little One after he had made his by now customary appearance at his appointed hour, Govinda addressed me in a somber tone. "Balu, I will talk to you regarding something that is very close to you, and which you consider as your last resort to provide you solace and comfort in the aftermath of first Grandma, and then Grandpa's demise. I am referring to the noblest of human relationships; Friendship.

For someone like you, who chose to remain a bachelor, and don't have the comfort of an immediate family, a genuine friendship assumes great significance. A true friend is like a shining light, showing the way in the enveloping darkness of loneliness. A true friend is someone to whom you can bare your soul, and show your emotional vulnerabilities that one would generally not want to show to the world at large. It could be an aspect of social conditioning, especially boys who are trained by the dictum of "Men don't cry".

Given these social constraints, a true friend comes as a divine blessing. But at the frenetic pace at which we lead our lives, some of it dictated by the demands of a career, and attending to family, and the remaining to our compulsive need to be always occupied with something, finding a true friend who sets aside some time from the cares of career and family for a friend in need has become the rarest of rare cases. By this supposition, I am not at all saying that one who finds time amidst his/her familial and official responsibilities for a friend is a true friend, while one who isn't able to do so is not a true friend. That would be too simplistic a viewpoint.

During the course of your sixty years of life so far, you would have found that childhood friends fade as one steps into adulthood, and generally friends made during the course of one's career have a limited shelf life. A friendship between two individuals sustains for as long as they share the same wavelength, the same values, and the same worldview. But these aren't supposed to remain the same for all time to come. It is generally the case that one of the friends in a friendship decides to marry and start a family, which comes with its own set of duties and responsibilities. Sometimes, these can get so overwhelming that one just doesn't have the time and the energy to even think of a friend, let alone call a friend.

Given this scenario, which tends to dominate the social landscape of our times, and also that friends may be separated by time and distance, it comes as no surprise that the friendship that one thought to be true and lifelong, starts waning. Of the two who form a friendship, the one who is invested in the friendship and who witnesses this uncomfortable change, is alarmed and starts doing everything he/she can to revive the friendship, and give it the same vibrancy it once had. But despite all the best efforts put in, the friendship refuses to revive, and get off the ground. The one who is busy with family and career is oblivious to all that is going on in the other friend's mind and heart, and what is more important to realize is the fact the he/she is not what they were a few years ago at the start of a friendship. The Buddhist teaching of impermanence can be very useful to understand the ebbs and flows in a friendship. The Buddhist world view postulates that we as individuals change, and therefore, the relationships between individuals are also subject to change. And this does not exclude friendship as well.

The other friend, who still lives in the idyllic past, and holds on to the conviction that friendships are for life, is rudely awakened to reality when he/she sees the changes playing out right in front of his/her own eyes. What normally follows is harbouring grievances/recriminations against a friend who has chosen to move on. There could be other occasions wherein a misunderstanding could erupt between two very good friends. The one who has ostensibly caused the hurt and damaged the friendship tries his/her level best to bring the other friend on board. He/she is willing to put his/her pride and ego aside and issue one sincere apology after another to reclaim the friendship that is on the verge of breaking up.

There are times when better sense prevails, and the aggrieved friend is willing to give the other a chance, realizing that we are after all human, and it is very difficult to be human and not err. If this pleasant state of affairs were to come about, then, it is another shot at life and friendship for the one who initially caused the rift in the friendship. Having learnt his/her lessons well, he/she would ensure that the same mistakes aren't repeated again to the detriment of the friendship, which is central to their lives.

But such happy endings may not always be the case. There are cases, and which you Balu have also experienced in your life, where the aggrieved friend has closed his/her mind to a reconciliation despite the best of efforts made by the other friend. The erring friend leaves no stone unturned by setting aside one's pride and ego, and tendering apology after apology for protracted periods of time. But even despite this long vigil, the friendship fails to regain the vibrancy of old. The friendship now resembles a garment so frayed that no amount of a strong stitch can cause the frayed edges to stay together, and will cause them again to tear within a short time. This is symbolic of a friendship that has outlived its shelf life.

The wise and mature thing to do for a friend who is in the dock is to make reasonable efforts at a reconciliation over a reasonable length of time. During this time, one shouldn't stop short of making any number of apologies if that can mean regaining the faith and confidence of an aggrieved friend. If despite all this, the aggrieved friend doesn't come on board, then one has to take the painful decision of letting the aggrieved friend go. This may sound difficult to stomach at first, but eventually, it will work best for both of them, and it is in their interests that they move on.

There can be cases in which the two parties to a friendship have differing levels of investment in a friendship. While one may be invested in the friendship just enough to consider the other a friend, the other owing to his/her nature and social circumstance may be invested more in the friendship, seeing the other as a true friend. These differing perceptions between two friends in a friendship will at some time lead to dissonance in the friendship, causing stresses and strains. While the one who is guarded in the friendship expects the other to respect his/her boundaries, the other one, who has chosen to impute greater value to the friendship by seeing the other as a true friend, tends to be more open in his/her communication, forgetting the fact that the invisible boundaries in any relationship shouldn't be crossed.

And when this mode of behaviour sustains over a period of time by the one who sees the other as a true friend, there comes a time when matters come to a head and the friendship goes downhill. There is nothing to be gained in mutual recriminations, which is not going to help either one's cause. The graceful option available for one who is more invested in the friendship is to realize his/her folly, and apologize for his/her transgressions. If matters settle down, and both are invested to the same degree in the friendship hereafter, there is occasion to rejoice. But it they don't, in spite of the best efforts made by the errant friend to reconcile, the wisest thing to do would be to cherish the friend and the friendship for the time it held strong, thank Providence for blessing one with such a wonderful friendship for the time it endured, and regretfully and painfully, take the difficult but necessary decision to move on.

Seen from the viewpoint of a soul's journey determined by the karmic blueprint that the soul choses before it incarnates on earth, friends that we make at different stages of our lives do not come randomly into our lives. They come into our lives to help us learn important karmic lessons, thereby enriching our lives and making it more meaningful, and when we have learnt our karmic lessons, it's time for them as well as us to move on. It is but natural that one develops a strong attachment to a dear friend, and to ensure the upward, evolutionary trajectory of a soul, even this attachment to a friend too has to be snapped, and that is what generally transpires.

If one sees friends and friendships from this rarefied viewpoint of a soul's evolutionary journey, he/she will view the friend and the friendship for the time it endured with a lot of affection and gratitude. And when the moment of reckoning comes, the process of letting go becomes relatively easier, though it will still be accompanied by the initial pain of what feels like losing a part of oneself.

So, dear Balu, my advice to you on friendship is this. Hold on to a dear friend with hoops of steel, as the Great Bard put it so finely in Polonius' advice to his son. And when a friendship starts showing signs of fraying, or one side of a friendship seems to be going off on a different tangent, giving rise to the feeling that the friendship is becoming one-sided, with one side doing all the heavy lifting of keeping in touch, it's time to hit the pause button. I would not advice one to call off the friendship, but do everything in one's capability to keep the friendship going.

And when there arises friction in a friendship due to wrongs committed, perceived or actual, it will not do the perceived or actual wrongdoer any harm to set his/her pride and ego aside, and tender a sincere and heartfelt apology. And allow a cooling off period. If after this, things come back on track, everyone's the better off for it. But in case the friendship shows no signs of reviving even after the cooling off period, then I guess it's time to gently let go, notwithstanding the pain and desolation it can cause. It is time for everyone concerned to feel thankful and grateful for the time the friendship lasted, and learn to move on, however difficult it may seem.

One should never make the mistake of unilaterally trying for long periods to correct a wrong. Pride and ego can be sacrificed to revive a friendship, but not one's self-respect. And when the stage of mortgaging one's self-respect to revive a friendship is reached, that is a clear sign that the friendship has run its course and it's time to gracefully move on, and thank God for blessing one with the friendship, and for the time it lasted.

Now, I know the question you have in your mind, Balu. What would happen when the only friendship I counted on as my support system shows signs of waning, the reality of which is difficult for me to accept?" Govinda looked at me with a lot of empathy and resumed in his sweet tone. "That day may also come, and you have got to be prepared for it. And if and when it materializes, you should have the inner strength, and grace to accept it without any trepidation, thank Providence for the time the friendship lasted, and learn to move on."

I interjected, "Govinda, what will then fill the void that is left in the aftermath of the ending of a friendship". Govinda resumed in a voice that is so very characteristic of a child of four or five, and in his case, a very sweet voice. "Don't worry. Haven't you built up a huge library of books at home, with books on Science, Mathematics and Spirituality, with books on Spirituality dominating your collection. Many of those books haven't been read yet. Start reading them, and it is my confident assertion that you can continue reading those books for the remainder of your lifetime.

And then, there is your first and enduring love that has been going strong for the last fifty-three years. I am referring to your love for Cricket. Follow the game, sharpen your insights, and may be, your next book should be a cricket afficionado's tribute to this glorious game. Grandpa watching from above will be thrilled and happy, for his love for cricket was no less, and had he put his mind to the game, he would have gone on to excel in it as well. Spend time on weekends at old-age homes, chatting up with senior citizens in the evening of their lives, who sometimes feel forlorn and yearn to see their children, who for various reasons may not be around. Be their child, albeit for a short while, and put a radiant smile on their faces, for nothing can match the noble endeavour of caring for the elderly, and making them happy. Revive your childhood passion for gardening. You have a green thumb, and you will see yourself forming a special bond with Mother Nature. See, you already have so much on your plate that the prospect of missing a dear friend gradually fades from your consciousness. Life has to be lived with a lot of grace. Try it, and you will be infinitely better off. Today's conversation on battling loneliness has been a particularly long one. I have eaten into your sleep time, and it is time I take your leave, and return yet again for another invigorating conversation".

Saying so, Govinda bade me goodbye, making me eager and enthusiastic for my tryst with my cherub the next day.

Stalling Spiritual Progress

Even before I could put my question to Govinda, he had already read my mind after keeping his date with me at his customary hour at night, and addressed me endearingly. "I know what you feel deep inside you regarding your spiritual progress. The feeling of an utter sense of disappointment, which makes you almost give up on your spiritual journey, marked by more failures than successes in your sixty years of life that you have led so far.

Let me deconstruct this erroneous assessment that you have made of yourself regarding your spiritual progress. Let me first of all talk about the popular perpetuated myths that persist among the large majority regarding spiritual progress. There is a school of thought that says that entering a thoughtless state where the mind doesn't generate any thoughts is the acme of spiritual progress. Now, let's put this under the lens, and see the merits of this postulate.

The first step in understanding the aforesaid postulate is understanding the nature of the mind. It is a tool provided by Providence for surviving, existing, and functioning efficiently in the world. The mind analyses, compares alternate sets of options, and chooses one, which provides the best choice with minimum tradeoffs. This analytical function of the mind requires it to take sensory inputs from the external world, process them, evaluate them, and generate a course of action as the output of its synthesizing function. In this state, it is but natural for the mind to generate a multitude of thoughts as part of its analyzing, synthesizing, and evaluating function.

As we transact with fellow humans in this world, it is but natural for the mind to generate thoughts, without which it won't be possible to exist and function in this world. Another domain of the mind is generating and dealing with emotions. Now, what is a human being sans emotion!! We could as well deal with an automaton. Human emotions span the range from happiness, grief, fear, love and many more. Human emotions enrich our lives, and provides an existential context to human life and progress.

To therefore say that emptying the mind of thoughts and emotions is the pinnacle of spiritual progress seems a flawed premise. Even aspiring to achieve this unrealistic state is fraught with disastrous consequences. The mind is a tool for our efficient functioning in this world, and it is but natural for the mind to generate thoughts and emotions.

The key to efficiently managing our mind is not to get entangled and attached to the thoughts and emotions that it generates. To be able to efficiently carry on our transactions with the world we inhabit, thoughts are a natural consequence. The problem with thoughts emerges when we associate and identify ourselves strongly with a particular school of thought, leading to ideological rigidity in politics, and fanaticism in religion. When it comes to emotions, this complete identification with emotions and consequent entanglement with them is equally fraught with harm; harming oneself and harming others. What was supposed to make us uniquely human by feeling and expressing emotions has become a curse. When human expression of love is not reciprocated, or there is a betrayal in love, it does cause pain to the one who expressed love to the other. But it shouldn't result in rage, and crimes of passion as has become more or less the norm now. Uncontrolled anger similarly can have terrible consequences, such as road rage cases on the rise, which can in some cases, result in loss of lives.

Now, let's examine why these aberrations occur. It is only because we have chosen to strongly associate ourselves with, and identify with our thoughts and emotions. We have thus chosen to live in our minds, and once this happens, we should be ready for the rollercoaster rides that the mind invariably is going to take us on, be it concerning our thoughts or our emotions. It is particularly so with emotions, when individuals get carried away by their emotions, and emotional highs and lows become more often than not, the norm, and not an exception.

Now what is the solution to these pressing human problems. The solution lies in cultivating a certain distance with respect to our thoughts, emotions and feelings. In other words, we have chosen not to live in our mind, but have made the wise decision to get out of our mind. If this skill is acquired, a human being becomes a witness to his mind, and there will always be a momentary pause between a thought and an action of such an awakened individual. He/she has chosen the Golden Mean of walking the Middle Path, and not easily excited by ideological debates, or aroused by one's emotions.

I can see that you have developed this ability to a reasonable extent with The Divine's blessings, though, I dare say that there is still a lot of scope for improvement from you. There are still times when your responses are almost immediate, not even pausing to reflect and understand what the other person is trying to convey. And when peace returns, you end up looking rather sheepish. So, work more on this area. My concluding advice to you is to skillfully use the mind as a tool, not become a tool to be manipulated by the mind. This is one big step forward in an individual's spiritual progress. You have made reasonable progress here, but much more can still be done by you. And you will be the wiser, and better off for it.

Now let us examine the second marker of spiritual progress, which has come to find a place in the collective consciousness of people. Reading spiritual biographies and autobiographies, one often comes across a spiritual aspirant experiencing the superconscious state with the blessings of his Guru. It is said to be a state beyond the mind, and therefore incapable of being described in words, as words happen to be the tools of the mind in describing an external or internal phenomenon. But one thing many spiritual aspirants have in common in describing this superconscious state is feeling ecstasy or indescribable bliss. This state teaches them the oneness of creation, and that the same spark of The Divine exists in all of us as individual souls. Having experienced this state, the sense of separation dissolves, and with this, ego and the little sense of "I" that a human develops also disappears, which feeds much of the struggle and strife that a human experiences. There is thus no sense of separation, as I and the world, or I and you.

This absolute sense of oneness is generally considered as a concomitant of spiritual enlightenment. Achievement of the superconscious state is earmarked for those few rare souls, who have progressed spiritually across many lifetimes, and finally reach the end of their spiritual quest. They have put all their energies to achievement of this state, which takes them beyond the endless cycle of births and rebirths. This exalted state cannot be the lot of everyone in this world. I am not saying that the spiritual potential isn't there in every human now on earth. The potential to reach this state is very much there in all of humankind, but there are very few who even think of spirituality, let alone spiritually evolve.

As I said earlier, the karmic blueprint that a soul chooses at the time of birth determines its soul journey in this lifetime. And if a soul has already put in the hard yards in a previous lifetime, their karmic blueprint will accordingly chart out their spiritual path and their spiritual journey in this lifetime. But for those like you Balu who are eager to evolve spiritually, but are not very consistent with their spiritual efforts, and lose heart very soon, I am now going to tell you multiple markers of spiritual progress, and if one has made reasonable progress on these spiritual markers, I would consider them to have made significant progress on the spiritual path. And they need not measure their spiritual progress just on one marker of spiritual enlightenment.

Let me elucidate these spiritual markers one by one. Let's start with empathy first. A human being who is empathetic is able to put oneself in another person's shoes, and see the world from his/her perspective. If one is able to put oneself in the position of the less privileged among our fellow human beings, he/she will be able to deeply appreciate the problems and the lot of people, who may be struggling to make ends meet and support their families. If one has resources, one can always apportion a small portion of their resources to helping the less privileged in the challenges faced by them. The cultivation of empathy is therefore followed by the cultivation of kindness and compassion, which makes us see the suffering of the less privileged as our own suffering, and extend a helping hand out to them. Any human who has made significant progress in cultivating empathy, compassion and kindness has progressed on the spiritual path. The true test of empathy, compassion and kindness is giving away a part of your resources, which you had earmarked for spending or buying something of special interest to you. And yet you don't bat an eyelid in setting aside your own interests for the larger and higher good. And measured on this parameter, you have progressed a fair bit. Take heart.

Let us move on to the second marker of spiritual progress. How often have we lost our temper, and said and done things, which we regret later. Angry words once directed at another can never be taken back, and it not only hurts the person at whom they are intended, but ends up leaving a residue of pain and regret with the one who couldn't keep a tab on his/her anger. Frequent bouts of anger can fracture human relationships within families, and between friends as well. A wise soul will practice enough awareness to immediately become aware of anger arising in his/her mind. And this precious awareness will give the practitioner of awareness a precious second or two to pause, and it is in this momentary pause that the wave of anger that had initially arisen falls and dissolves as well. It is important therefore to practice awareness of our mind, and identify the mental triggers that give rise to anger. Bo doing so, one can stop anger right in its tracks. Balu, it makes me happy to say to you that you have progressed very well in reining in your anger.

Another obstacle to spiritual progress is in being oversensitive to another person's critical observations about oneself. A wise one would hear out the critical observations of a friend or colleague, and accordingly respond, assuring the other of corrective measures in focusing on one's areas of improvement. More often than not, most of us tend to have an inflated opinion of ourselves, and a critical observation from a well-wisher stings our ego, and pricks the bubble in which we tend to live. And in a manner of getting even, we angrily react to this feedback in a defensive reaction. This is what stops us from improving ourselves, and condemns us to remain where we are. Setting one's ego aside, and being all ears to hearing someone give feedback to us calls for a large heart, and an acceptance that we aren't perfect, and are willing to work on ourselves. You have a long way to go here, Balu. Though you feel you have reined in your ego to a reasonable extent, you get offended easily when someone has a point of view not in agreement with yours. You don't angrily retort, but start reacting by putting out statements to the effect that what you did was in good faith. You don't have to be so defensive. Just listen. And then see what is it that you need to do to correct your behaviour. If you are able to do this, you would have taken one big step forward in your spiritual evolution.

Standing by a friend in his/her time of need is another significant step forward in your spiritual evolution. Lending an ear to a troubled friend, and offering him/her gentle counsel is something very noble. In today's time and age the convenient excuse of many is they don't have time for anything. Setting aside time and energy to hear a friend unburden his/her soul, always being there for a friend, whatever be the time of day, and whatever be the circumstance are gestures that keeps the flame of genuine friendship burning bright and strong. This is a marker on which you have done very well.

Caring for one's aged parents is perhaps the most important milestone in one's spiritual journey. As our parents gather on in years, and struggle with their daily routine; as their children, it is our bounden duty to take care of them, and attend to their needs. Regular visits to the doctor, getting their tests done, and helping them out in household chores does make a significant difference in easing their burden. There are times when this onerous responsibility does test our patience, and quite often, we lose our temper and snap at them. But remorse comes visiting to the wise child, who on realizing his/her mistake is the first person to apologize and seek forgiveness from one's parents. The Divine takes a very considered view of this very important role that can quicken one's spiritual evolution, and spur them forward on the spiritual path.

There is something I wish to speak to you, Balu. It may come as unsolicited advice, but I will nevertheless say it, as I am very concerned about your welfare and well-being. Two areas where you are lacking in, and need to put in a lot of work are attachment and craving. Craving can either be gross or subtle. Grosser cravings tend to be physical, such as craving for food, sleep, and something I don't need to tell you about. You know it pretty well. Put in sincere effort in seeing the emptiness and futility in these cravings. Suppressing these cravings isn't the solution to the problem. Maturity lies in watching with awareness these cravings arise and fall in the mind, while not getting entangled with them. It is in watching these cravings with awareness that one learns to distance oneself from them, and gradually, with practice, there will come a day when these cravings fall off on their own.

Subtler cravings take the form of attachments that we tend to develop for an idea, an object, or a person. Here too, we should train to use our Consciousness as a witness to these attachments that the mind in concert with the ego tends to form. The mind in tandem with the ego, its ever-willing collaborator, tricks us into believing that it is human to form attachments. I am not at all positing that one shouldn't have any attachments at all, for it is love and attachment that keeps a family structure strong and vibrant, and also serves as the fuel that keeps friendships going. All that I am trying to say is that attachments shouldn't become inordinately strong, for that is when strong attachments suffocate and smother relationships, within a family and without. So, it is important to know the threshold within which one should stay as far as attachments go.

The one exception to attachments is deep love and attachment for The Divine. If one can develop it during one's lifetime, it is almost like a benediction from The Divine. And since parents are considered the closest to divinity, there are no limits to the amount of love and attachment that one can have for one's parents, sobered by the realization that there will come a time when they will pass on, and we should retain our objectivity and our mental balance to accept the inevitable gracefully.

And if this love for family and friends can become universal and unconditional, it is one giant step forward in one's spiritual evolution. These exalted states of human consciousness don't materialize all of a sudden; it isn't as if you wake up one day transformed. That isn't how spiritual progress occurs. It takes lot of effort in working on oneself, having the courage to unflinchingly look at oneself in the mirror, warts and all, and consistently work on improving oneself, while at the same time being gentle on oneself. Any kind of evolution is a slow and gradual process, and one should be patient with oneself.

In conclusion, I would like to reiterate that on quite a few markers of spiritual evolution, you have done reasonably well. But there are a few areas that require more effort for you to register significant progress therein. Keep working on yourself, putting your faith in The Divine. Let The Divine be the sole judge to decide when you are ready for the state of spiritual enlightenment. And my parting shot to you is only when you empty yourself will there be space for Grace to enter and transform you". With this, Govinda bade me goodbye, with his reddish palm and delicate fingers standing out conspicuously in the darkness of the night as he left the physical dimension.

I felt a deep sense of gratitude surging and coursing through my being, for this is what I was waiting for the Little One to speak and show me the way. And the Little One, as was his wont never disappointed.

Preserving Our Spiritual Heritage

As Govinda appeared once again at his appointed hour, and I sat up in my bed, agog with excitement to hear what he was going to speak about tonight, Govinda looked at me, more radiant than ever. It was as if the topic that he was going to speak about gave him a lot of happiness, and this happiness seemed to add to his lustre as he addressed me thus.

"I am going to speak about something that is very dear to you. And which you have been doing for nearly a decade and a half now. It is a practice that is held to a high standard in almost every religion, and particularly so in Hinduism, according to which it is the highest form of charity. I am referring to the noble act of feeding the poor and the hungry. Swami Vivekananda very rightly observed long ago that you cannot teach religion to a hungry human being. First and foremost, it is important to put away the fires of hunger that gnaws at every human being. And for those for whom putting food on the table for their families, or managing two square meals a day isn't such a problem, it becomes their prime duty to address this most important of human need, especially among those who are poor, and don't have the resources to eat even a single meal.

It is important to also address the important issue of food that is wasted almost every day. Whether it be marriages, social functions or gatherings, food is an integral part of human connection and celebration. Marriages or social functions do call for a celebration, but which should avoid the extremes. One shouldn't end up in a situation where the guests feel shortchanged when it comes to food, or the other extreme of an expansive food menu where food is offered at several counters by themes. I really wonder whether it is possible for people to eat so much. Even if the argument for such an expansive menu is in favour of giving lots of options for the large number of guests in attendance, one can still see that the options to eat border on the excess.

Often times, out of sheer gluttony, people pile enough on their plates as a preemptive move not to miss out on anything subsequently, only to realize later that there is only so much their stomachs can accommodate, and end up leaving uneaten portions on their plates, which ends up in the dustbin. It has become customary for children to leave something uneaten on their plates. It is important that children are taught the importance of food, given that there are millions of fellow humans who go without a morsel of food many times. They need to be sensitized enough to the fact that the food that is on their plate needs to be respected and honoured, and that the food that they chose to waste could have filled up a hungry person's stomach.

Similarly, the elders while planning weddings and other family functions should refrain from switching to either of the extremes, and choose a menu that addresses the palate of a large cross section of invitees. And not go overboard with excess when it comes to hosting and entertaining guests.

It gladdened my heart no end when I saw you perform Annadanam on Rama Navami day, the birthday celebrations of Lord Rama. It also happened to be the observance of the monthly date (thithi) of Grandpa's passing, and since Lord Rama was Grandpa's idol, you couldn't have chosen a better day to perform Annadanam. And you have heard Grandpa recount with pride how his own parents would celebrate Rama Navami in a grand manner, inviting workers from the railway yard to come and have lunch that they would serve plentifully and generously.

As we grow older, it is important for us to realize that rather than indulge ourselves with clothes and gadgets, which we can well do without, it would indeed be a noble turn of heart to instead spend this same amount of money to serving food to the poor and the hungry. Sri Ramakrishna Paramhansa very aptly said that we should serve food to the hungry with no sign of pride, but complete humility. We should thank the receiver for having given us an opportunity to serve him/her. Sri Ramamkrishna advised us to see God in the poor and hungry when feeding them, and Annadanam at Ramakrishna Math is appropriately titled Narayanaseva.

Another important aspect of our spiritual heritage that we need to preserve are the rituals performed by priests at the time of Upanayanam, marriage, child birth, death etc. These rituals are detailed in the Agama Shastras that dealt with different types of rituals, worship, construction of temples et al. I do concede that priests make exorbitant monetary demands for their services, and it is becoming increasingly difficult for people of limited means to perform the death ceremonies of a dear one such as one's parents. If people out of sheer economic desperation give up the performance of these rituals owing to lack of financial resources, it is understandable. But people who have the means should perform these rituals. It has become a fad amongst the educated lot to mock and poke fun at these rituals. If one is well versed in these Agama Shastras, and sees priests cutting corners, or performing rituals half-heartedly, and censures them, then I fully stand behind such a brave individual. But if one mocks these rituals without even understanding the spirit behind them, and operates out of ignorance of these rituals, then it is not right at all.

The new generation of priests is dwindling, as children of priests get a modern education, and pursue disciplines closer to their heart. There are a few noble initiatives wherein Acharyas start Vedapatashalas, where boys from poor Brahmin families are taught not only the Agama Shastras, but also modern education, while also providing them free boarding and lodging. This is one last big attempt to ensure that our spiritual traditions are kept alive. And Grandpa fully understood the importance of these Vedapatashalas, and expressed his desire to contribute a significant amount to a Vedapatashala started by Shri Velakkudi Krishnan, who left a flourishing corporate career to devote his life to preserving and spreading Sri Vaishnavism. I was so happy that you took time off to personally go down to Srirangam, and meet Sri Velakkudi Krishnan to hand over the amount that Grandpa wished to contribute to his Vedapatashala.

When it comes to preserving our spiritual heritage, what matters isn't the quantum of contribution. What matters is the spirit in which such initiatives are undertaken, and love and joy in one's heart when contributing one's mite". With these concluding remarks, Govinda left me with a very cryptic remark, "Tomorrow is going to be an exhilarating day. And also marks my last visit in these series of visits and conversations with you".

I was left puzzled, as to what the Little One had in mind, which was going to make the next day exhilarating. With these thoughts occupying my mind, I drifted off into the realm of sleep. A realm that at least temporarily keeps you blissfully unaware of the real world, and gives the much-needed respite for mind, body and spirit to rejuvenate themselves.

Flight to Redemption

For arguably my last conversation with Govinda, and what he had promised was going to be exhilarating, I was left guessing as to what the Little One had in mind. I therefore went through my daily routine with a lot of gusto, having my eyes constantly on the clock to see when the appointed hour would draw near. Nearly thirty minutes before 10:00 pm, I was sitting in bed, and counting down the minutes to the appointed hour.

Exactly at 10:00 pm, the Little One materialized right before me, as he had done so many times before. But his chubby countenance had a mirthful smile, the purpose of which I wasn't able to discern. Before I could ask him any further questions, he addressed me in his sweet, childlike voice.

"Balu, I am going to take you on an exhilarating journey tonight. You need to be brave, and follow my instructions very carefully. I know what is in the deepest recesses of your heart. Just close your eyes, and hold my hand while we together embark on this exhilarating journey. Have complete trust and faith in me. Since I am a being of light, appearing before you in my astral form all along, I have to temporarily appear in my corporeal form so that you get a real feel of holding my hand", he chuckled mischievously. Slowly the light form filled out to reveal the three-year old Govinda, the child I loved so dearly, conversed with, and played with. The same ruddy complexion, the same chubby countenance, the same black and magnetic eyes, the same little, sharp nose, and the jet-black tuft of wavy hair that sat atop his head. I was beside myself with joy and held him in a warm embrace. After a few moments of experiencing the bliss of embracing Govinda, he asked me. "Shall we embark on what is going to be a fun journey?" he said in his characteristic mischievous tone. I said Yes.

I held his gentle and ladylike hand, which I remember kissing and playing with. The same pink palm, the same slender, delicate and tapering fingers. I clasped his right hand tightly, closed my eyes, and told Govinda that I was ready. The Little One's exultant tone couldn't be missed as he responded to me with "Off we go".

I got the feeling of ascending through space, as I had to keep my eyes closed. Even with my eyes closed, I knew that there was no light source around, as that would have caused my eyes to perceive a dash of orange even when closed. After quite some time had elapsed, I got the feeling that my body felt lighter than its usual weight, which the force of gravity invariably and naturally creates. I therefore realized that we had transitioned from the physical dimension to a different dimension that wasn't governed by the physical laws of the universe.

Even with my eyes closed, I could discern that we had entered a dimension of light, as my closed eyes could easily sense ambient light all around. After traveling in this dimension for some time, I got the feeling that we were finally alighting at the end of this exciting and pulsating journey. Govinda asked me to open my eyes, and as I did so, I found myself in an ethereal dimension that was far removed from the grossness of my earthly existence.

A certain feather-like lightness had permeated every dimension of my being; physical, mental, emotional and spiritual. I felt that I had entered a realm whose predominant theme was one of bliss. Govinda told me that we needed to walk some distance in this wonderland that I seemed to have entered. Still holding Govinda's hand, I walked with him for a distance, after which we came to a clearing. There loomed in front of me a beautiful architectural wonder, an imposing building meant to house people, I thought to myself. Govinda asked me to wait at the gate, while he entered the building. He was gone for quite a while, and my anxiety seemed to build, alone as I was in what seemed to be alien land to me. As if reading my anxiety, Govinda stepped out of the entrance to the main building and walked towards me, his countenance suffused with joy and happiness. Behind him walked two astral beings, and since they were at some distance from me, I couldn't make out their contours and guess as to who they were.

As they came nearer, my curiosity reached a crescendo, and I couldn't contain my excitement, as I could feel the pounding of my heart, and my pulse racing. They seemed to be older people as their silhouettes came much within my visual range. I could clearly now discern that they were an old couple. An aura of light seemed to surround them, and they seemed to be dressed in flowing white garments. The old gentleman was draped in a white dhoti and a flowing white kurta, while the lady appeared dressed in a white sari and a white blouse. I had my heart in my mouth as they came closer. To my utter wonder and amazement, my deceased parents were standing right in front of me.

I almost fainted from this pleasant shock, but Govinda held my hand and steadied me just in the nick of time. Govinda said, "See, I have brought you the two people you were longing to see; Grandma and Grandpa. They are now in their spirit form after casting off their mortal coil. Bearing the infirmities of the human body is no longer their cross to bear any more. For a brief while, I have sought permission from The Divine for them to assume their corporeal form. It will last till your rendezvous with Grandma and Grandpa".

Saying so, Govinda urged me to get closer to my parents. As I saw them in full view, and very clearly, the pent-up emotion of missing them made me prostrate myself before them in a gesture of complete love and respect. It was my father who as was his wont, kept his composure, strode towards me with his adroit gait, bent down, lovingly held me by my shoulders, and asked me to get up. As I stood up, my father's first spontaneous gesture was to envelop me in a warm embrace. The days, weeks and months of loneliness and desolation was washed away the moment he held me close to his chest. In his characteristic firm voice, he addressed me, "Balu, I know what you have been going through for the last several months. I have been watching over you along with your dear mother fighting off loneliness, and struggling with an overwhelming sense of desolation and emptiness. I do agree that all this is a necessary part of grieving. I have also seen you feeling guilty sometimes. Feeling a sense of guilt is also a part of grieving, my dear son. It is not an experience unique only to you. Everyone goes through this smorgasbord of emotions in the aftermath of a bereavement. I have seen you walk into our room, and seeing the emptiness pervading there, leave with an ache in your heart. We both were worried that you would drown in this grief and sorrow of having lost both of us. We cannot reenter the physical realm to calm you down, reassure you that everything will be fine, and that you should take heart and make an honest and sincere effort to move on.

We were earnestly hoping that you would dig deep, find your inner reserves of strength, and draw on them to come out of the period of grieving that is a rite of passage for almost everyone who has parents. After almost forty-eight days of grieving, you finally pulled yourself together, and made peace with reality. Both your Mum and I heaved a huge sigh of relief at our little fellow finally picking himself up, and learning to stand on his own two feet all alone in this world. That was what had us worried no end as to what would become of you when we were gone.

My heart swelled with pride as I saw you attend to all my affairs with a certain adroitness and determination that I hadn't seen in you while we were alive. Getting my death certificate, closing my accounts at the Post Office and the Bank, terminating my LIC policy, and carrying out your duties honestly as the Executor of my Will was extremely heartwarming and satisfying to both of us. The advice that I always gave you that once you take on a responsibility, you should not rest until it is successfully completed finally came alive as you went about attending to my work with a quiet determination and a fierce intent. This was seen in how you steeled yourself to complete all the demanding paperwork that my erstwhile employers IGNOU asked you to complete in order to process my pending medical reimbursements.

Let me assertively state with a lot of pride that you did everything a son could for an ailing father. Right from the time I was diagnosed with Ascites and my confinement to bed from mid-October 2022 – end-February 2023, you and your sister did everything in your capacity to attend to me, and help me deal with my illness. Yes, The Divine played an important role in orchestrating my recovery beginning March 2023, and my subsequent return to normalcy. And you became an instrument in the hands of The Divine in carrying out His will. There were times when I have watched you ponder over whether you could have done something more for me. Don't ever entertain that thought. The Divine out of its infinite compassion granted me an additional two years, and the privilege of becoming a nonagenarian. My time on earth was drawing to a close, and Existence has to create circumstances wherein the physical body gradually withers away, paving the way for the soul's ascension. With my life force becoming feeble with each passing day, my body in order to conserve itself withdrew from almost all activities, and retreated into a state of deep sleep. That explains why I kind of slipped into a deep sleep, unable to respond to your gentle entreaties to wake up and have something to eat.

And while you kept vigil by my side at the hospital, my little grandson, invisible to you all, was keeping vigil by my side from the spiritual dimension. My involuntary cry of Govinda reached his ears, and he was by my side in a trice, and helped me peacefully make the transition upon completion of my earthly journey. I didn't suffer at all, thanks to Divine Grace, and the support of my little grandson.

Son, I am extremely proud and happy at how you have handled yourself in the aftermath of losing both of us. It isn't an easy proposition to deal with the ensuing loneliness and desolation all by oneself. I am happy that you have handled yourself well. Continue supporting Radha in running Gurukulam in whatever capacity you can. From what I have seen of you, wield your pen to create public awareness about Autism, and other related conditions such as Down's Syndrome, and the special institutions that are called for to train the specially-abled, and integrate them into the mainstream of society. And continue being a moral support to Chellamma as she bravely undergoes treatment for her illness. I think I have said enough", and gesturing to my mother, he asked her to step forward.

My mother stepped forward with her slow, measured gait that radiated dignity. She came close to me, and held me in a tight, warm embrace. That yearning for human connection, which the heart yearns for in long spells of loneliness and desolation, finally materialized. And what better human connection than one's own mother, who stands unrivalled when it comes to the purity of her heart brimming with unconditional love for her children. My mother was not given to public displays of emotion, even with respect to her children. And I, who was basically an introvert, never ever gave my mother even half a hug, and this was something that had turned into a lifelong regret after her passing. I always kept kicking myself that I should have stepped forward and shown my affection to my mother.

As if reading my mind, she of her own volition came forward and enveloped me in a warm embrace. I held on to her tightly not wanting to let her go, the way I would done as a child of three or four. A mother's embrace carries with it the warmth of love, and makes you feel secure and cared for. More than five years of longing and yearning for my mother had finally borne fruit. She now addressed me in her gentle, low voice.

"Balu, please don't grieve over our loss. Both I and your father lived full lives, and you gave us no cause for complaint. You called time early on your career to spend quality time with us, and took on the household chores, which was becoming increasingly difficult for us as we carried on in years. You were there for us for our regular reviews with our doctors. And attended to every aspect of keeping us happy and comfortable. More than anything else, you gave us your undivided time and attention. We couldn't have asked for more. You have been a very obedient son, and watching you feel sad at our loss makes us sad as well. The laws of Nature apply to all without exception, and anything which is born has to die one day. So, please learn to gracefully accept the fact of our passing, and live the remainder of your life happily and purposefully. You are still careless with your eating habits, which worries me no end. Please have your food on time, do your exercise not excessively, but only what your body can bear. Aside from being happy, and making your life worthwhile, it is important for you to accord high priority to your health". Saying so, she stepped back and joined my father, who was watching the mother-son interaction with a lot of pride.

I once again prostrated myself in an act of complete surrender, love and gratitude. They gave me their bounteous blessings. Govinda, who was witnessing all this with his trademark mischievous smile, addressed me thus. "Balu, is your soul now at peace?" Have you finally found closure that you were looking for?". I said, "Not only closure, but given me immense joy at reconnecting with my parents, albeit in spirit form. I have finally felt a great load lifting off my soul, and I felt a lightness of being that I haven't felt in a long, long time." Govinda was all ears, and he finally said, "Shall we take leave of Grandma and Grandpa? Our time for leaving is drawing near. Grandma and Grandpa, I will see off Balu back to mother earth and then join you back here. Saying so, he again asked me to close my eyes, and hold his hand.

As I did so, I felt myself being transported from a realm of light. As we crossed over from the spiritual dimension back to space, which is the beginning of the physical dimension, I felt that joyful lightness of being giving way to a gradually increasing grossness associated with life on earth. This heaviness kept on increasing, and when we started alighting back to mother earth, I was back to feeling the way I used to feel myself on earth, subject as I was to the physical laws of the universe.

When I finally felt the hard ground beneath my feet, I knew that this fascinating journey of redemption for my soul had finally come to an end. Govinda now asked me to open my eyes, and there I was standing in my room, completely rejuvenated in mind, body and spirit. I looked at Govinda with deep love and gratitude, and said to him, "You came at just the right time when I was struggling with loneliness, desolation, and literally adrift in the sea of humanity around me. Your conversations have given me great clarity, and have cleared all the confusions, misunderstandings, and biases that were clouding my mind and my sense of judgement. I have one last question to ask of you. Will you come to me when my time draws near?"

Govinda looked me at me with great love and affection, and proclaimed in his gentle tone, "I will definitely be there for you when your time comes. But there is still a lot of time left for that. I know when your time ends on earth, but I am not allowed to share this with you now. And I am sure that after meeting Grandma and Grandpa, your life will have a greater sense of purpose and direction. You still have a lot to contribute to the cause of Gurukulam. Continue being a Good Samaritan like you have always been. And keep the flag of Grandpa's legacy flying high". Saying these comforting words, Govinda bade me goodbye, and disappeared from view.

I settled myself into my bed, and feel asleep in an instant. The way I had seen Govinda fall asleep when he was a baby. My healing process had well and truly begun.

Epilogue

In the aftermath of losing both my parents, I had to battle loneliness all alone. And in these moments of solitude and nostalgia, I would recall beautiful memories of my time spent with my parents. These memories would leave me with mixed feelings, at once making me treasure those fond memories, whilst also feeling a tinge of sadness that my parents were gone.

In these moments, I would venture into a dialogue with myself, and these dialogues are presented in the form of conversations with my Cherub, my nephew, and the apple of my eye. The first book, "Miracle – Conversations with a Cherub" was written in the aftermath of losing my mother. And the struggles that I went through post my mother's demise found expression in Miracle – Conversations with a Cherub.

Nearly five years after my mother's demise came the passing away of my father. This time, the challenge was even more daunting. While five years ago, I at least had the comfort of one parent still with me, this time round, I lost my remaining parent, my father as well. While my father was there to comfort me after my mother's passing, there was no one around me on a day-to-day basis to comfort me after my father passed away.

The empathy that I developed in attending to my father led me to conversations with my own self on various matters that were very close to my heart. And these conversations with my own conscience resulted in the current offering "The Return of the Cherub", which is in fact a sequel to Miracle – Conversations with a Cherub.

The writing of The Return of the Cherub has been cathartic for me, as immersing myself in a creative endeavour with my Cherub being its central and focal point not only gave me a great source of joy, but more important, provided me emotional closure.

I am sure readers who have already ready "Miracle – Conversations with a Cherub" will relate very well to The Return of the Cherub. For those who are yet to read Miracle – Conversations with a Cherub, I suggest that they read it first before venturing to read its sequel, "The Return of the Cherub".

Happy reading and introspecting.